BEGINNING TO END

Paper to Book

by Elizabeth Neuenfeldt

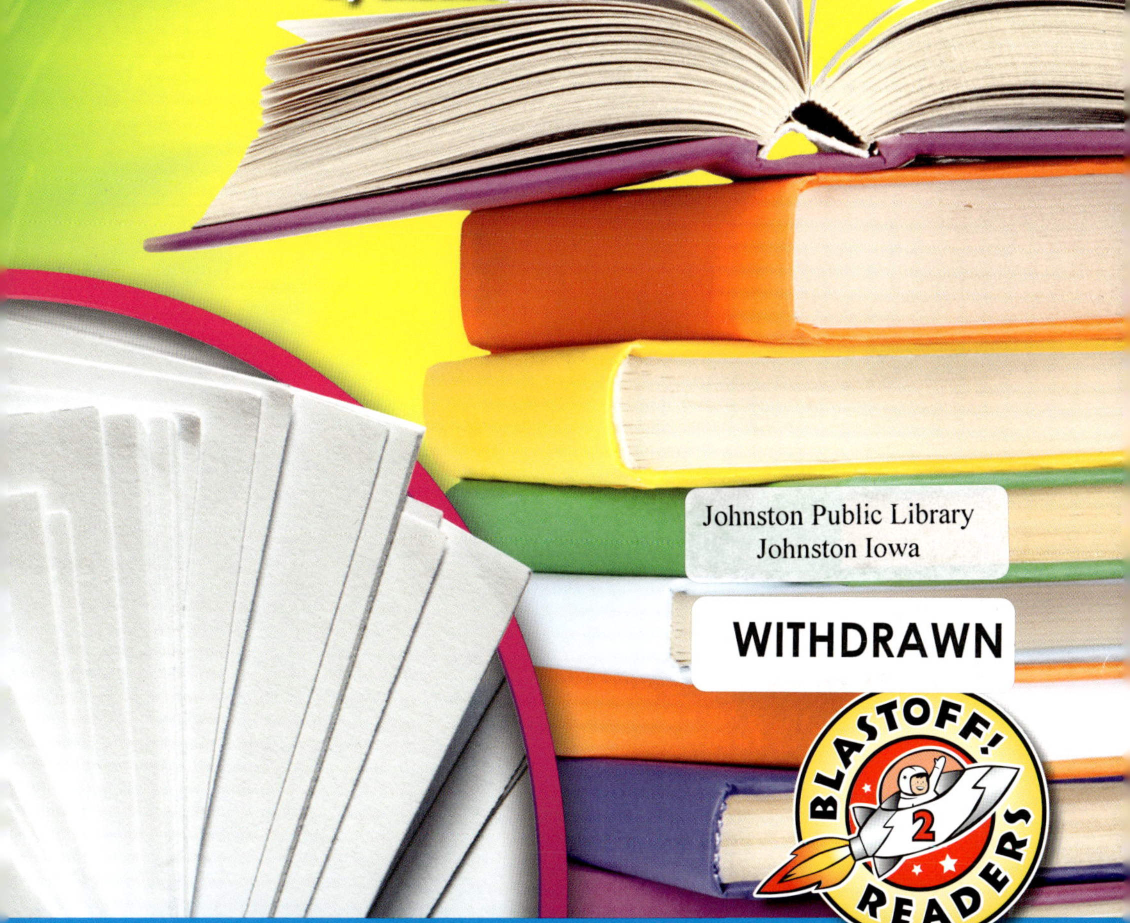

BLASTOFF! READERS 2

BELLWETHER MEDIA • MINNEAPOLIS, MN

Blastoff! Readers are carefully developed by literacy experts to build reading stamina and move students toward fluency by combining standards-based content with developmentally appropriate text.

Level 1 provides the most support through repetition of high-frequency words, light text, predictable sentence patterns, and strong visual support.

Level 2 offers early readers a bit more challenge through varied sentences, increased text load, and text-supportive special features.

Level 3 advances early-fluent readers toward fluency through increased text load, less reliance on photos, advancing concepts, longer sentences, and more complex special features.

★ **Blastoff! Universe**

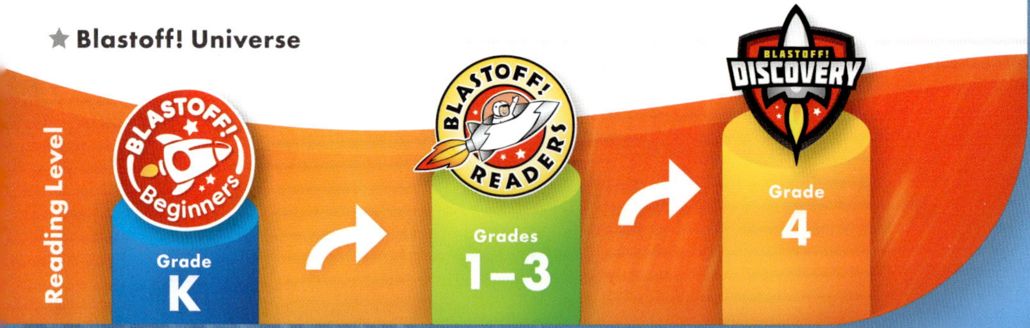

Reading Level:
- Blastoff! Beginners — Grade K
- Blastoff! Readers — Grades 1–3
- Blastoff! Discovery — Grade 4

This edition first published in 2021 by Bellwether Media, Inc.

No part of this publication may be reproduced in whole or in part without written permission of the publisher. For information regarding permission, write to Bellwether Media, Inc., Attention: Permissions Department, 6012 Blue Circle Drive, Minnetonka, MN 55343.

Library of Congress Cataloging-in-Publication Data

Names: Neuenfeldt, Elizabeth, author.
Title: Paper to book / Elizabeth Neuenfeldt.
Description: Minneapolis, MN : Bellwether Media, 2021. | Series: Blastoff! readers: Beginning to end | Includes bibliographical references and index. | Audience: Ages 5-8. | Audience: Grades K-1. | Summary: "Relevant images match informative text in this introduction to how paper becomes a book. Intended for students in kindergarten through third grade" Provided by publisher.
Identifiers: LCCN 2020039249 (print) | LCCN 2020039250 (ebook) | ISBN 9781644874233 | ISBN 9781648342455 (paperback) | ISBN 9781648341007 (ebook)
Subjects: LCSH: Books–Juvenile literature. | Bookbinding–Juvenile literature.
Classification: LCC Z116.A2 N48 2021 (print) | LCC Z116.A2 (ebook) | DDC002–dc23
LC record available at https://lccn.loc.gov/2020039249
LC ebook record available at https://lccn.loc.gov/2020039250

Text copyright © 2021 by Bellwether Media, Inc. BLASTOFF! READERS and associated logos are trademarks and/or registered trademarks of Bellwether Media, Inc.

Editor: Rebecca Sabelko   Designer: Laura Sowers

Printed in the United States of America, North Mankato, MN.

Table of Contents

Book Beginnings 4
Printing Papers 6
Binding and Trimming 12
Ready to Read! 20
Glossary 22
To Learn More 23
Index 24

Book Beginnings

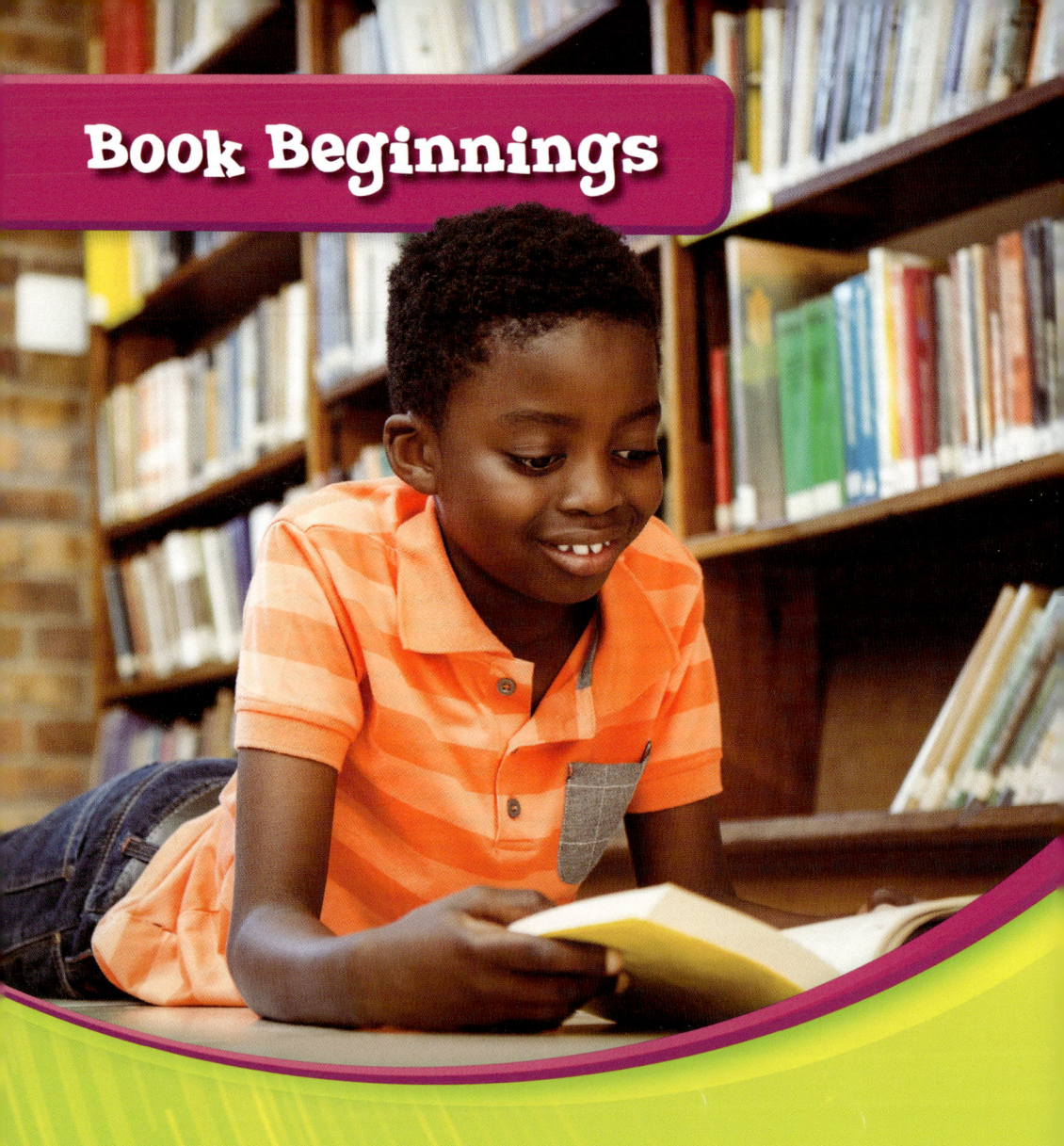

Have you ever wondered how books are made?

Where Was the First Book Made?

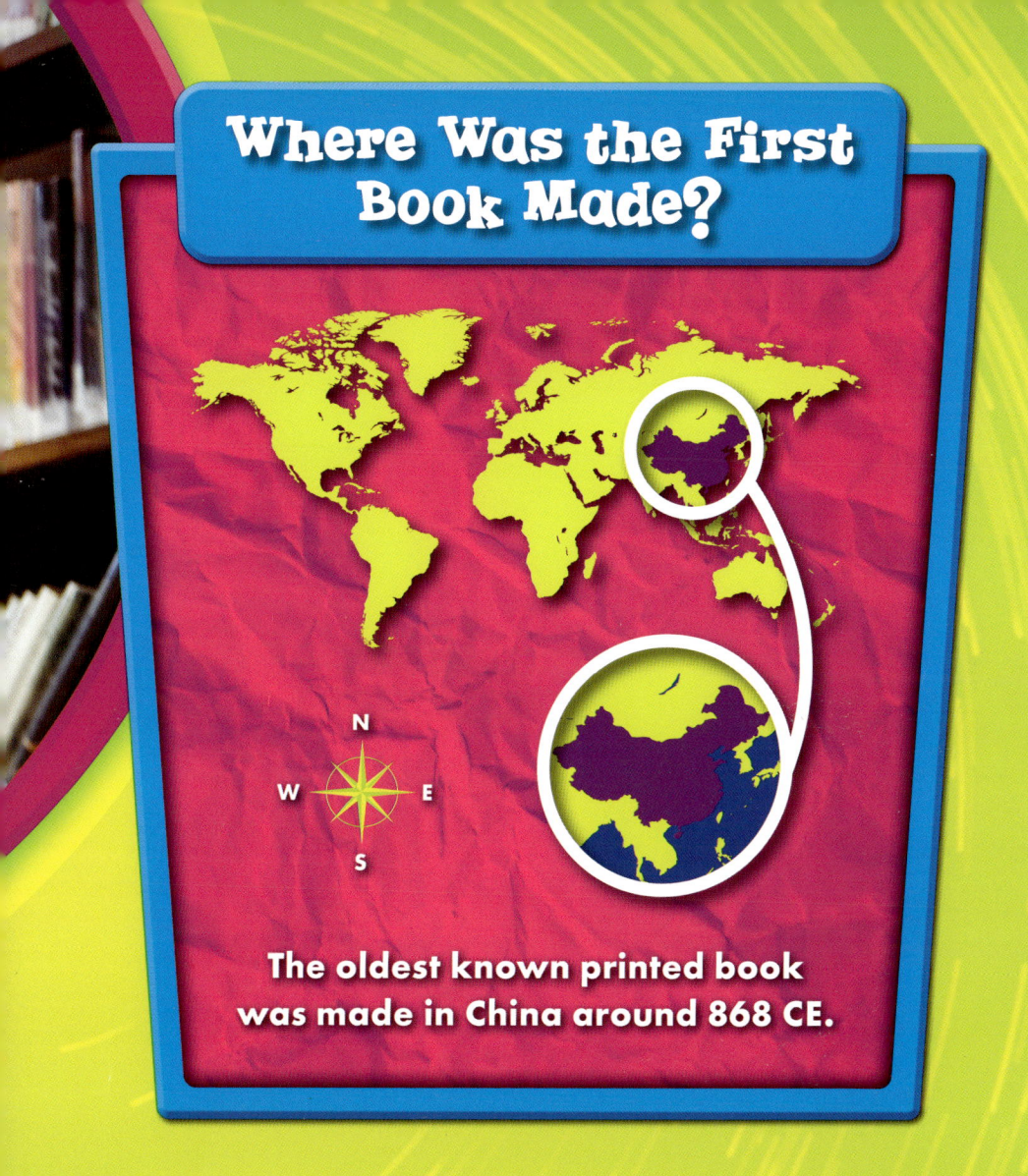

The oldest known printed book was made in China around 868 CE.

Books are made in factories. They begin as sheets of paper.

Printing Papers

metal plate

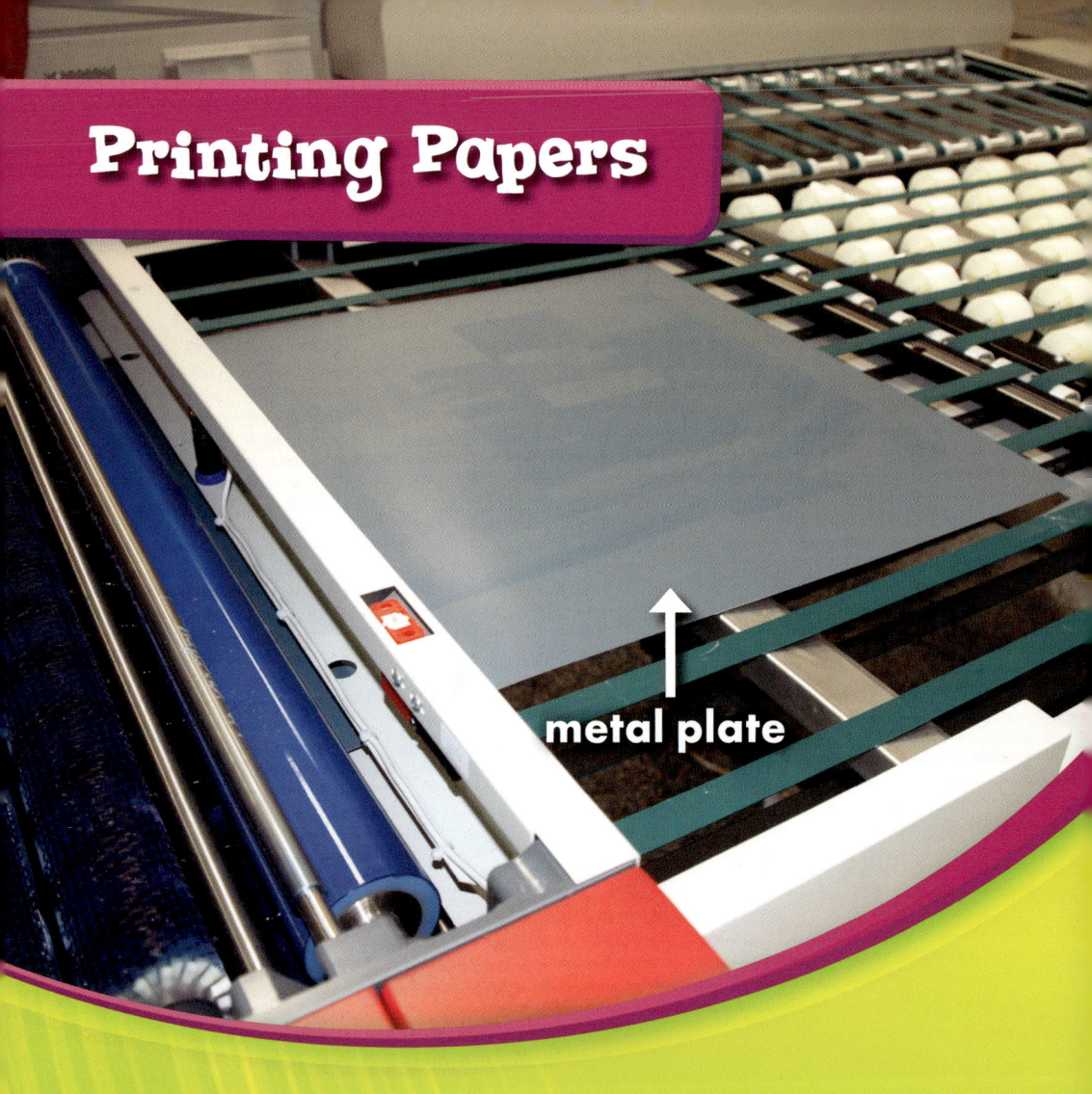

First, a book **layout** is sent to the factory. The pages of the book are copied onto metal plates.

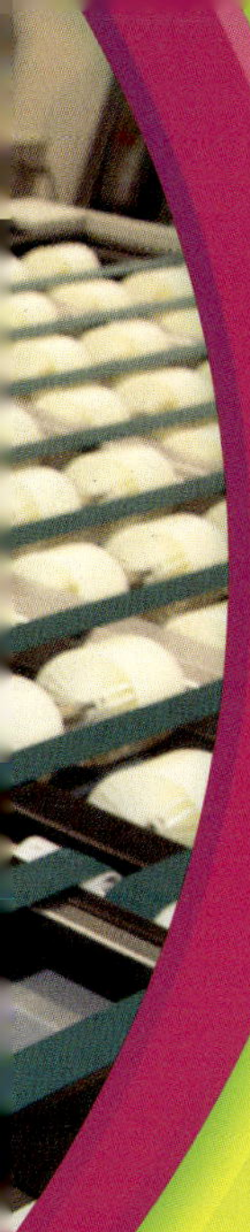

One plate can fit up to 64 pages!

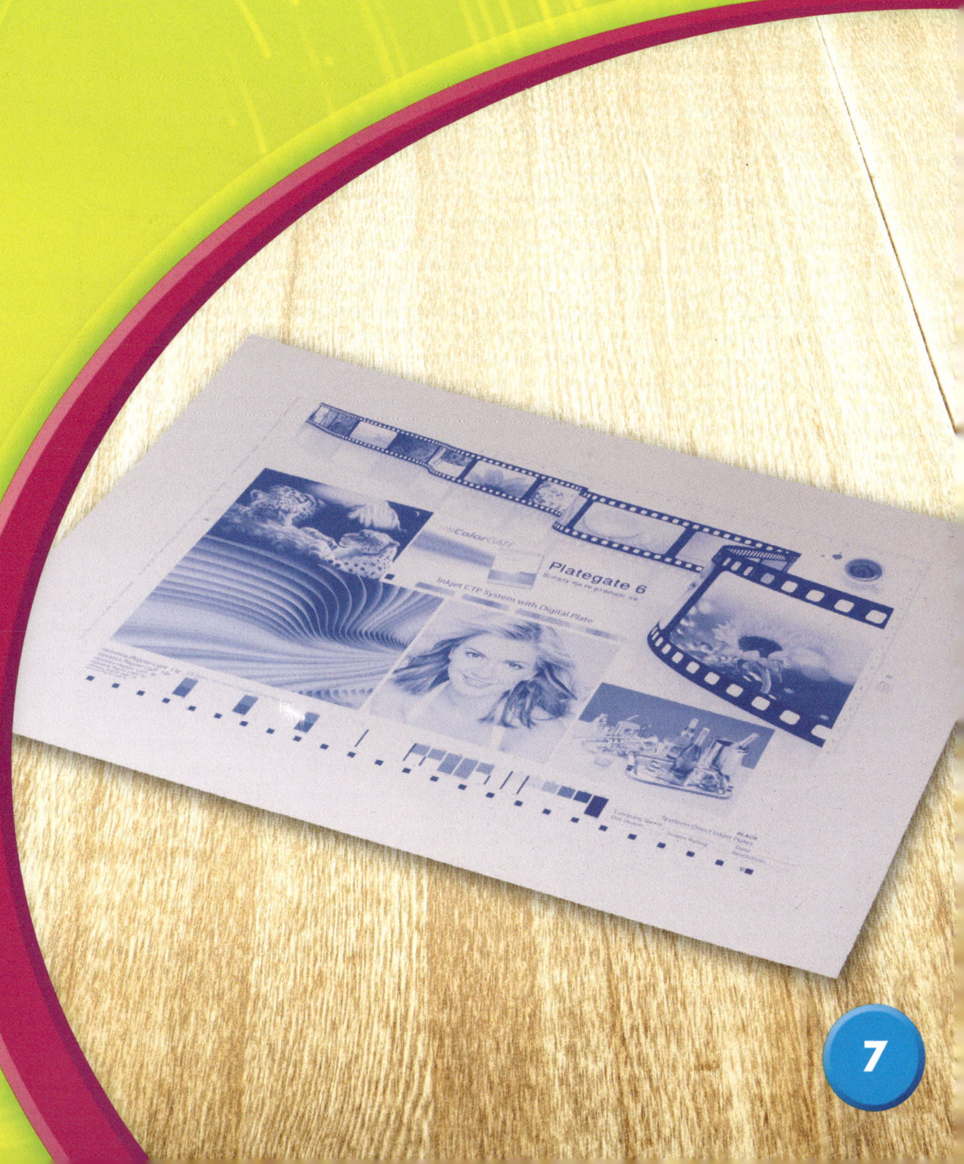
Plategate 6
Inkjet CTP System with Digital Plate

The plates are placed on a **printing press**. They are covered with ink.

Large sheets of paper move through the press. The pages are printed!

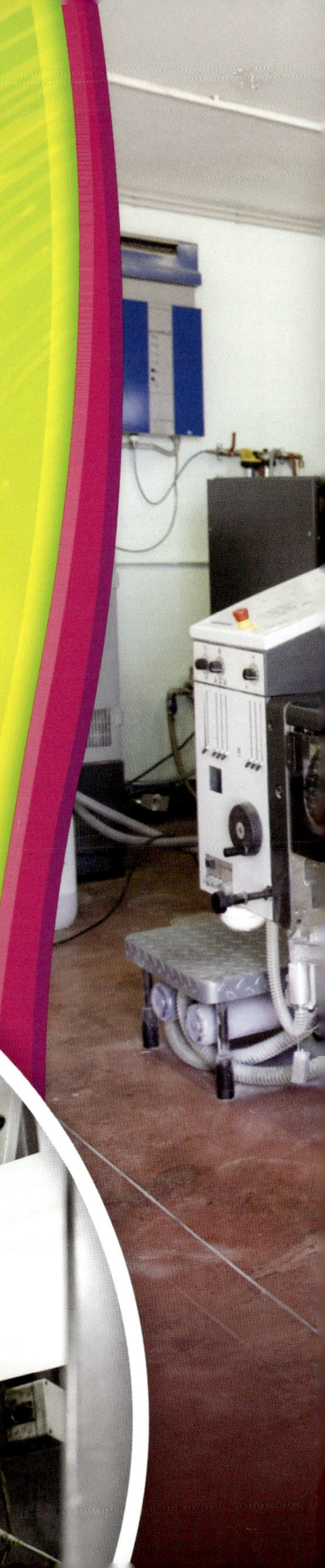

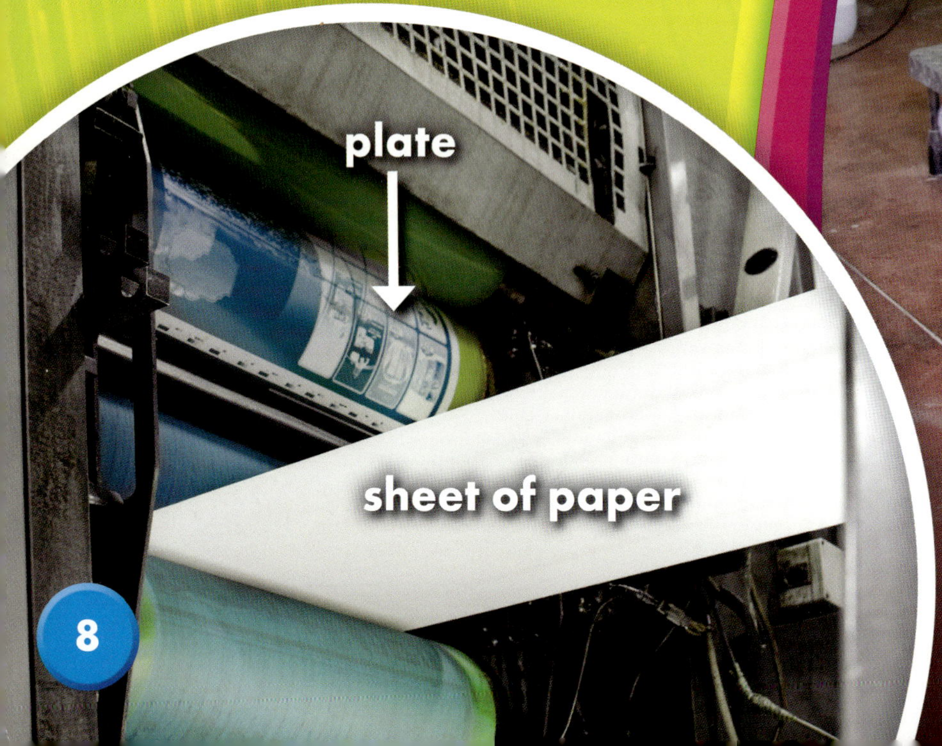
plate
sheet of paper

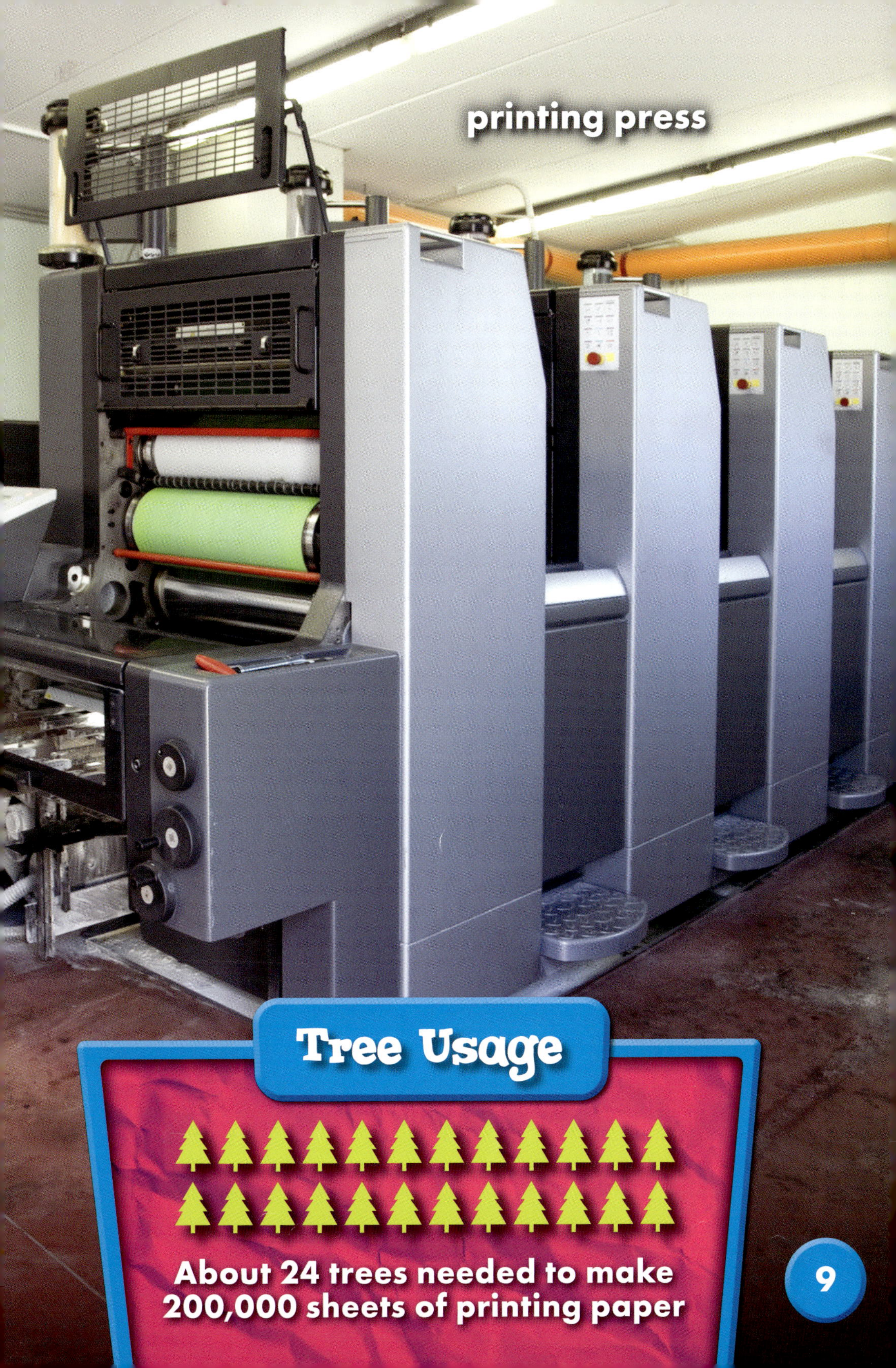

printing press

Tree Usage

About 24 trees needed to make
200,000 sheets of printing paper

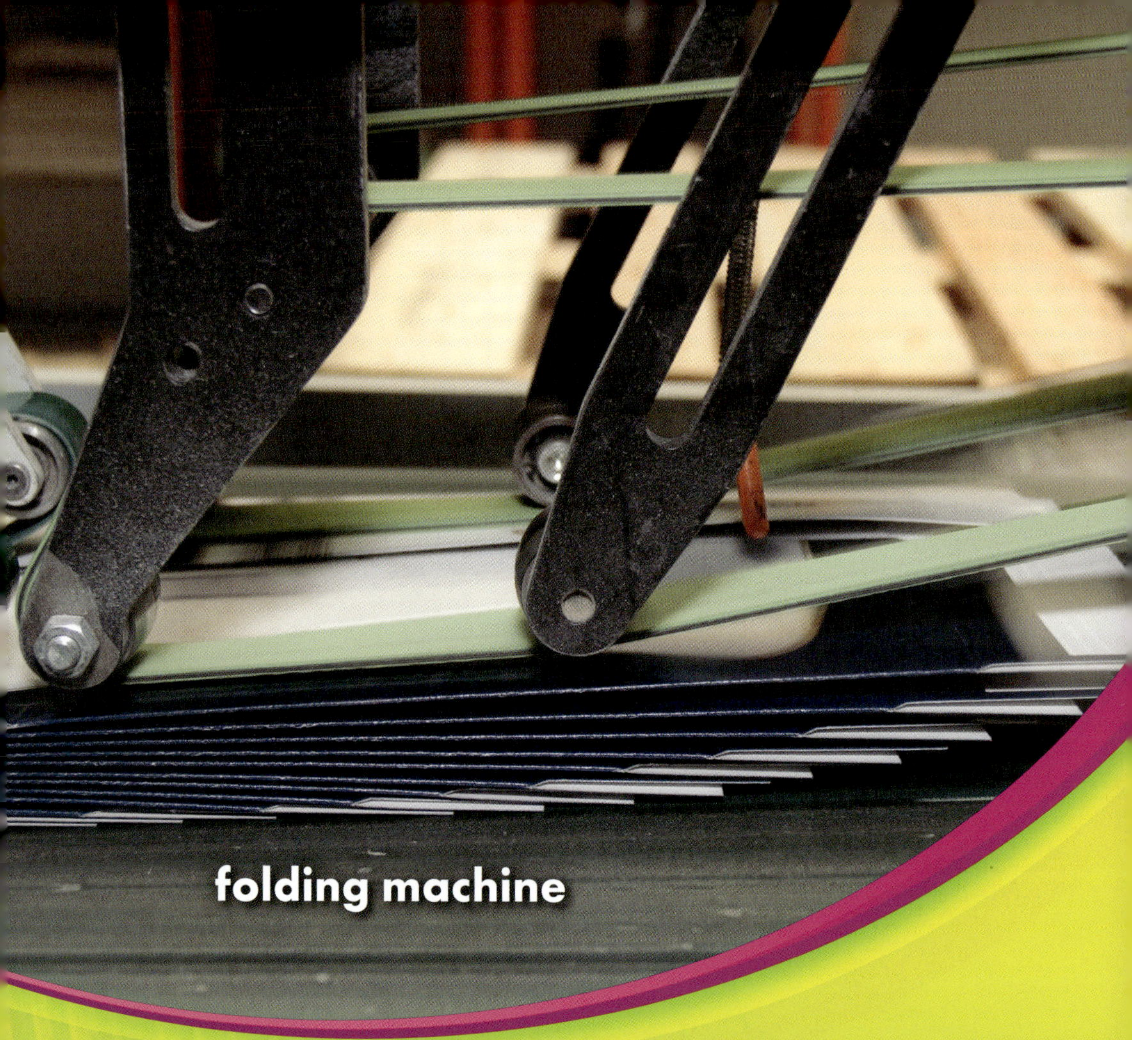
folding machine

The paper is cut into smaller sheets. These sheets go through a folding machine.

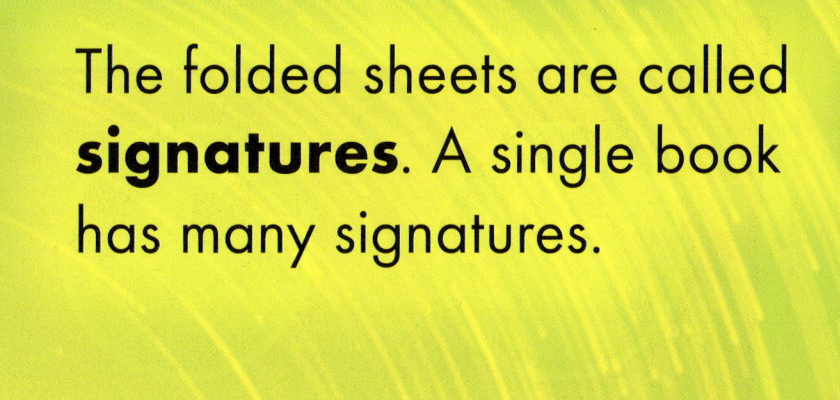

The folded sheets are called **signatures**. A single book has many signatures.

↑
signatures

Binding and Trimming

The signatures are sent to a **bindery**.

They are stacked in order. Then they move through a binding machine.

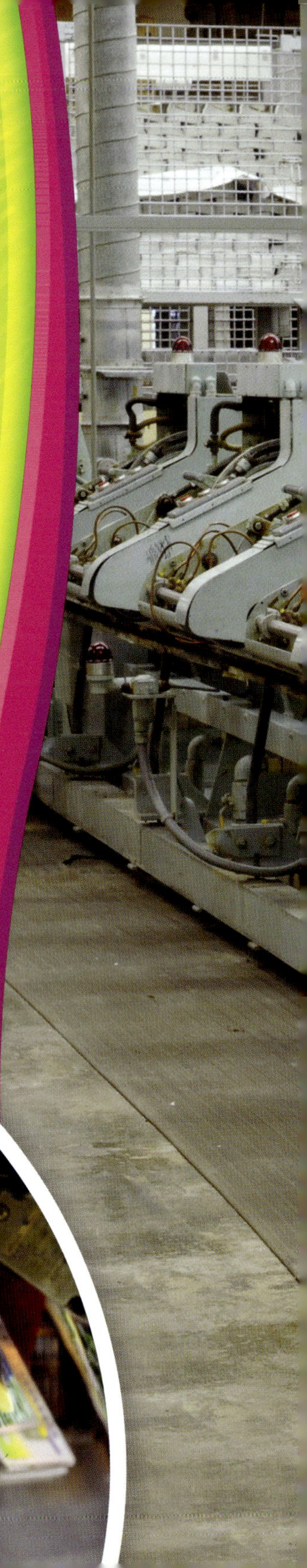

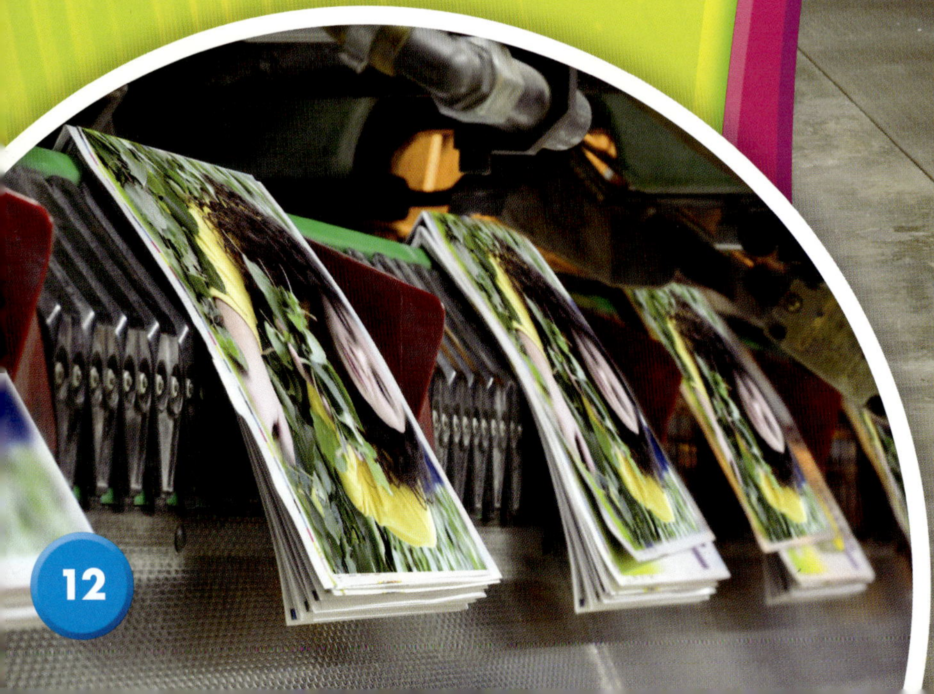

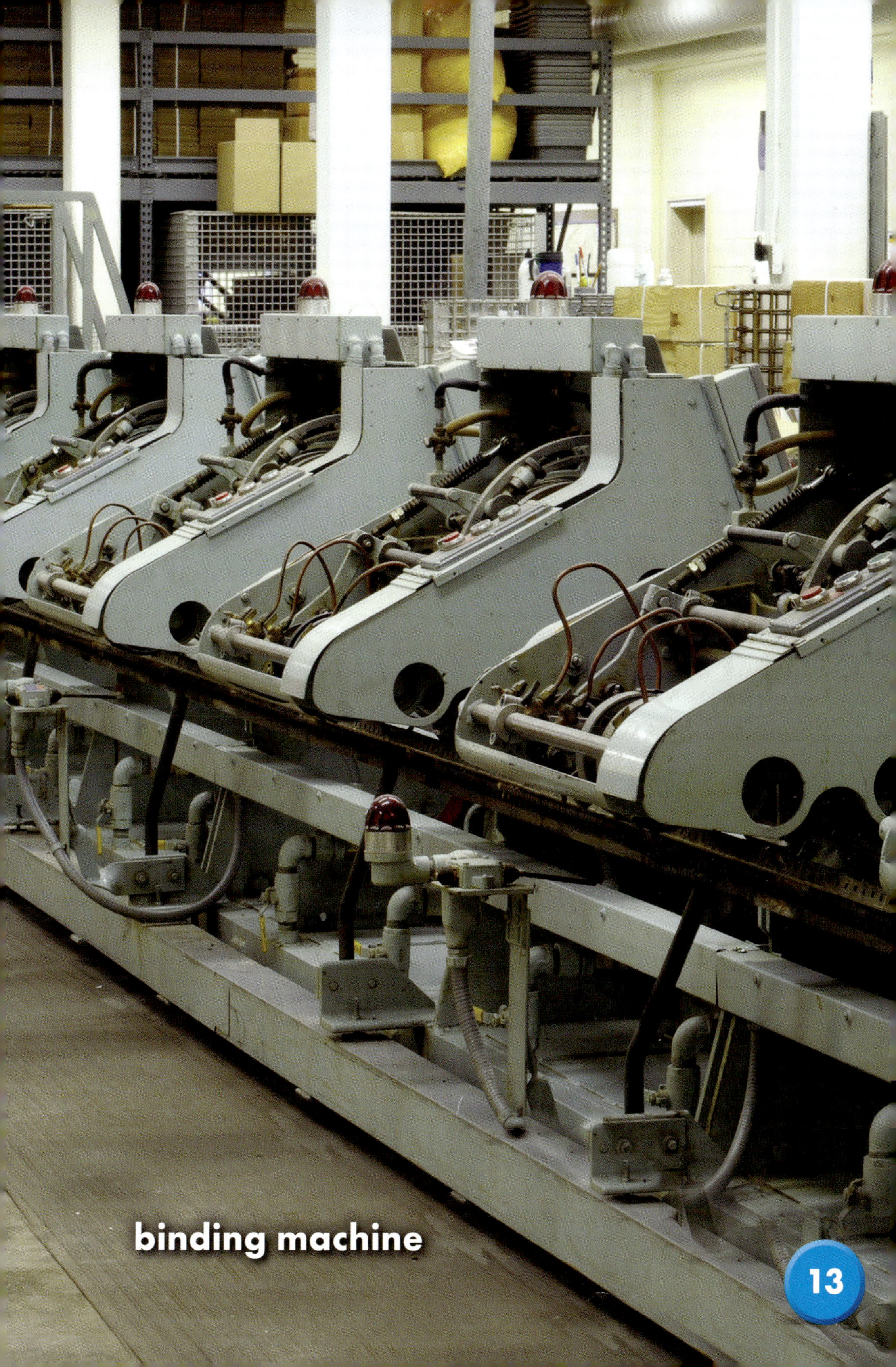

binding machine

The binding machine joins the inner edges of the signatures together.

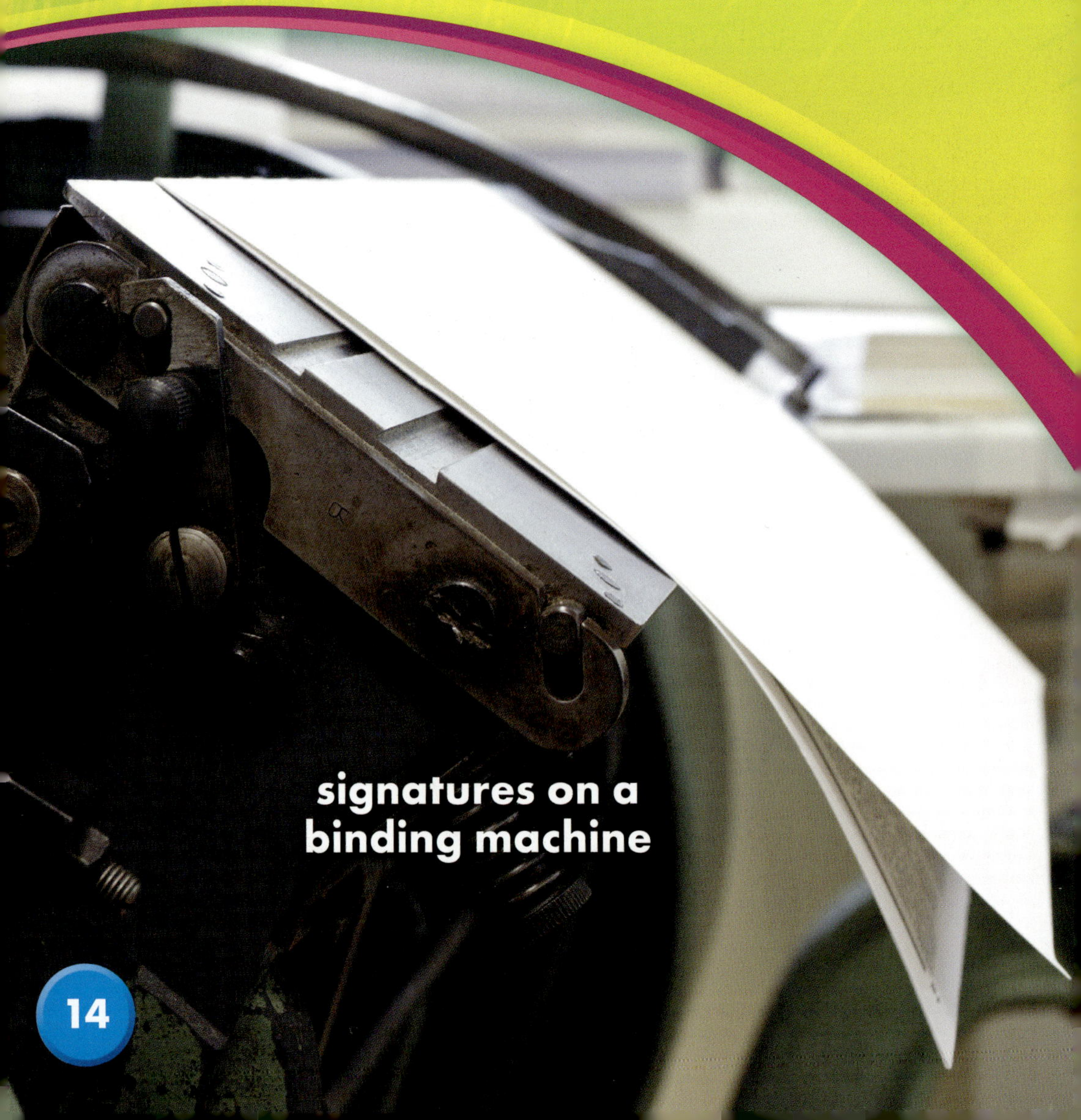

signatures on a binding machine

Binding Books

binding machine

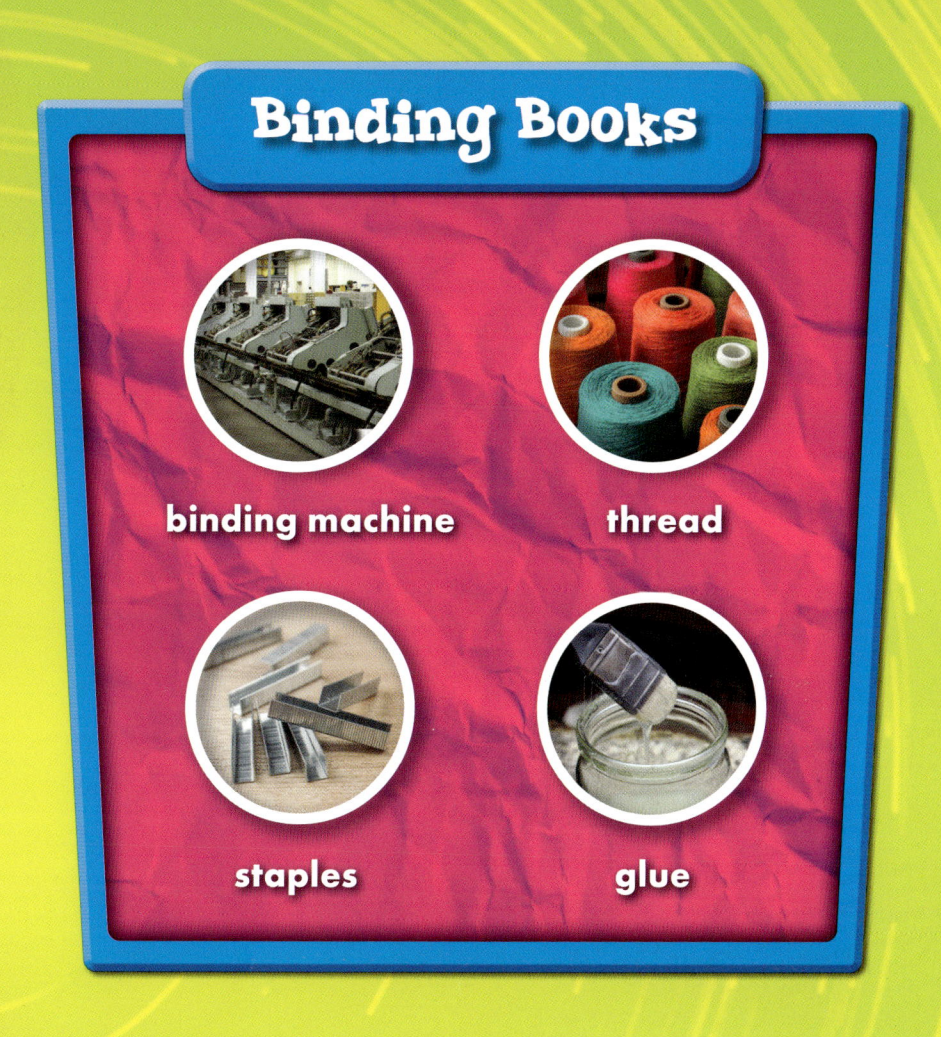

thread

staples

glue

Some signatures are sewed together with thread. Others are stapled or glued.

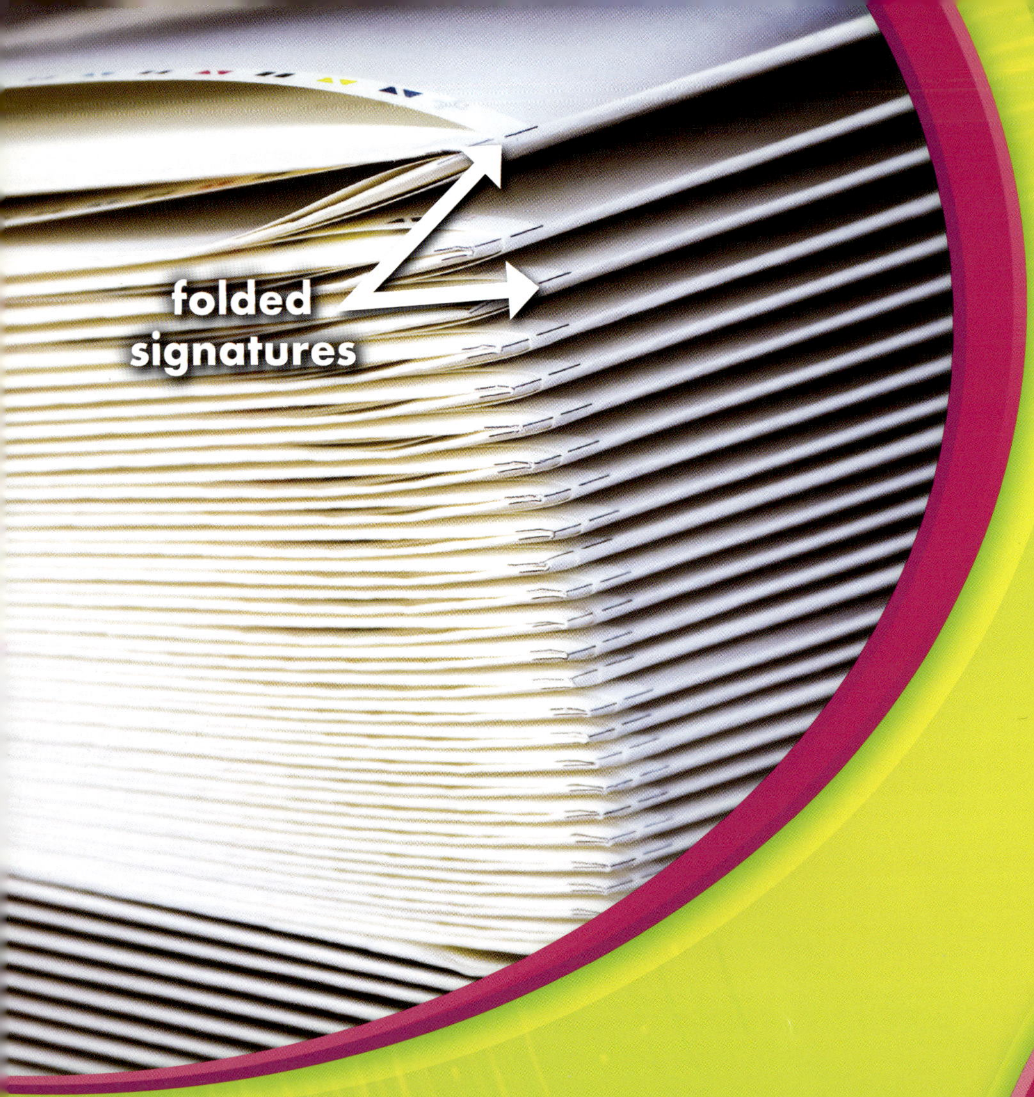
folded
signatures

After the signatures are put together, the pages do not fully open.

A **trimmer** cuts the folded edges of the signatures.

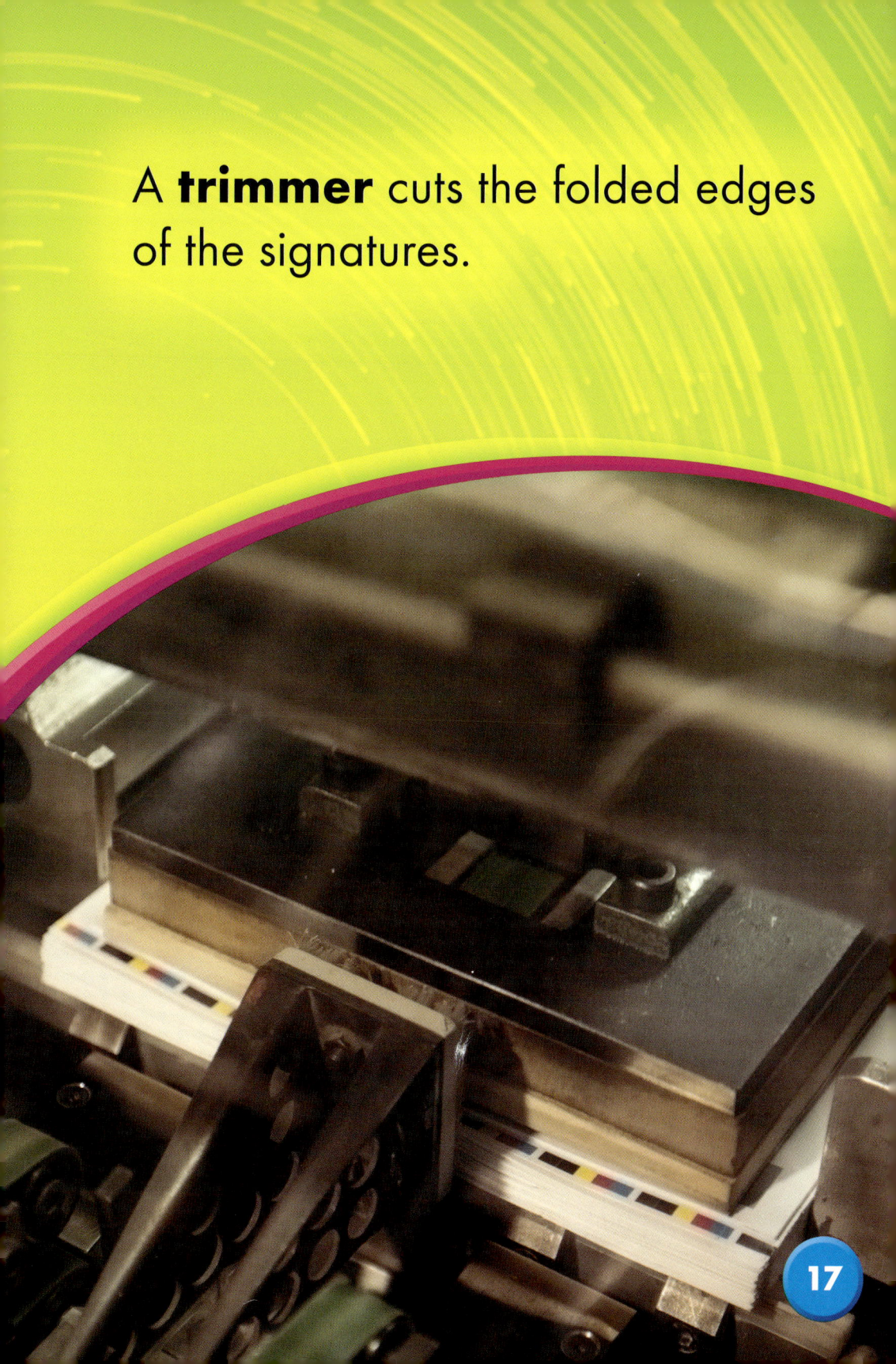

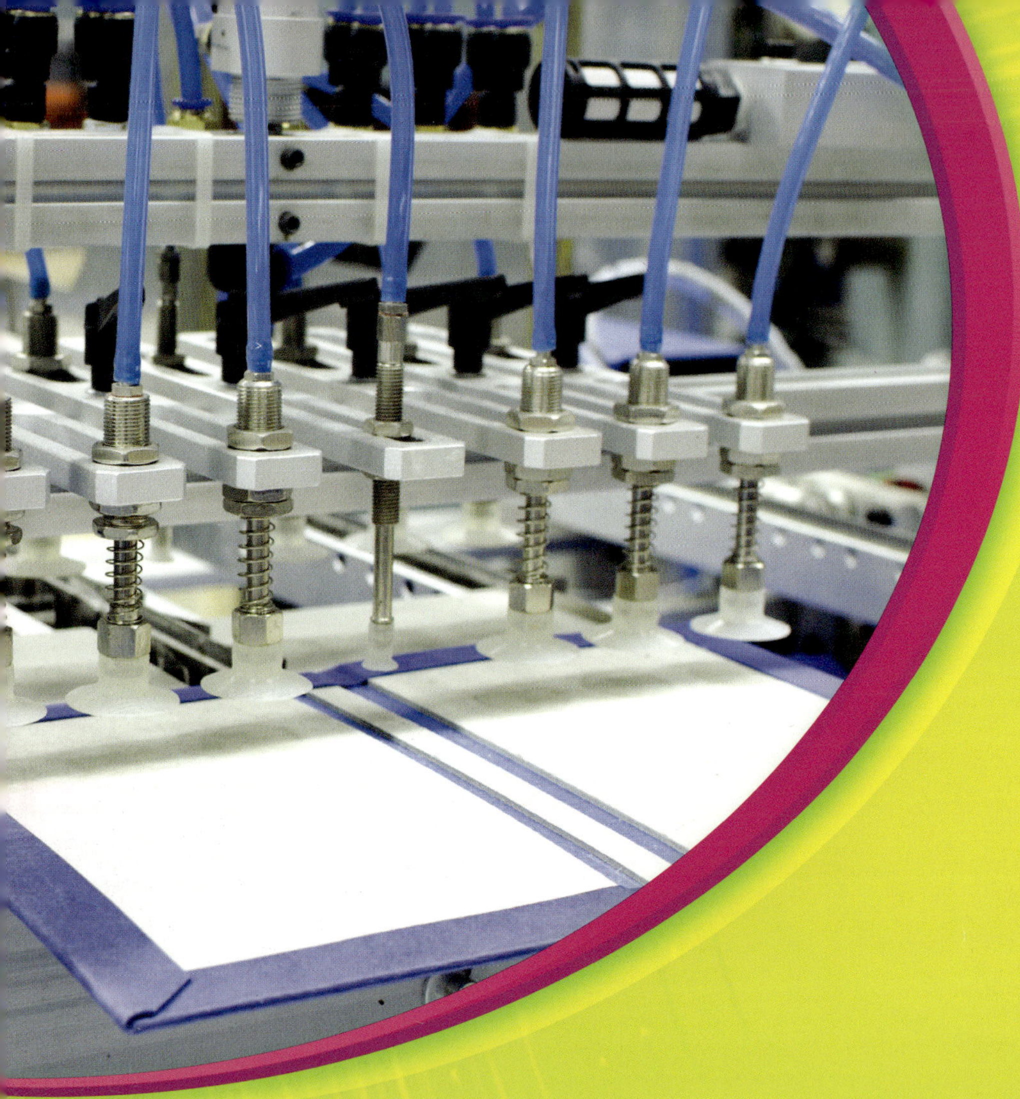

The books are ready for covers. A machine glues a cover to the front and back pages of the book. The book is ready to read!

Paper to Book

1. place layouts onto metal plates

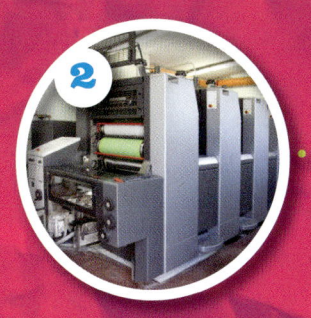

2. print pages using a printing press

3. fold paper into signatures

4. bind signatures

5. trim folded edges of signatures

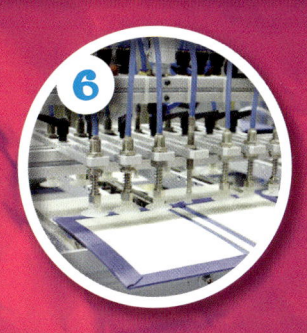

6. glue on covers

19

Ready to Read!

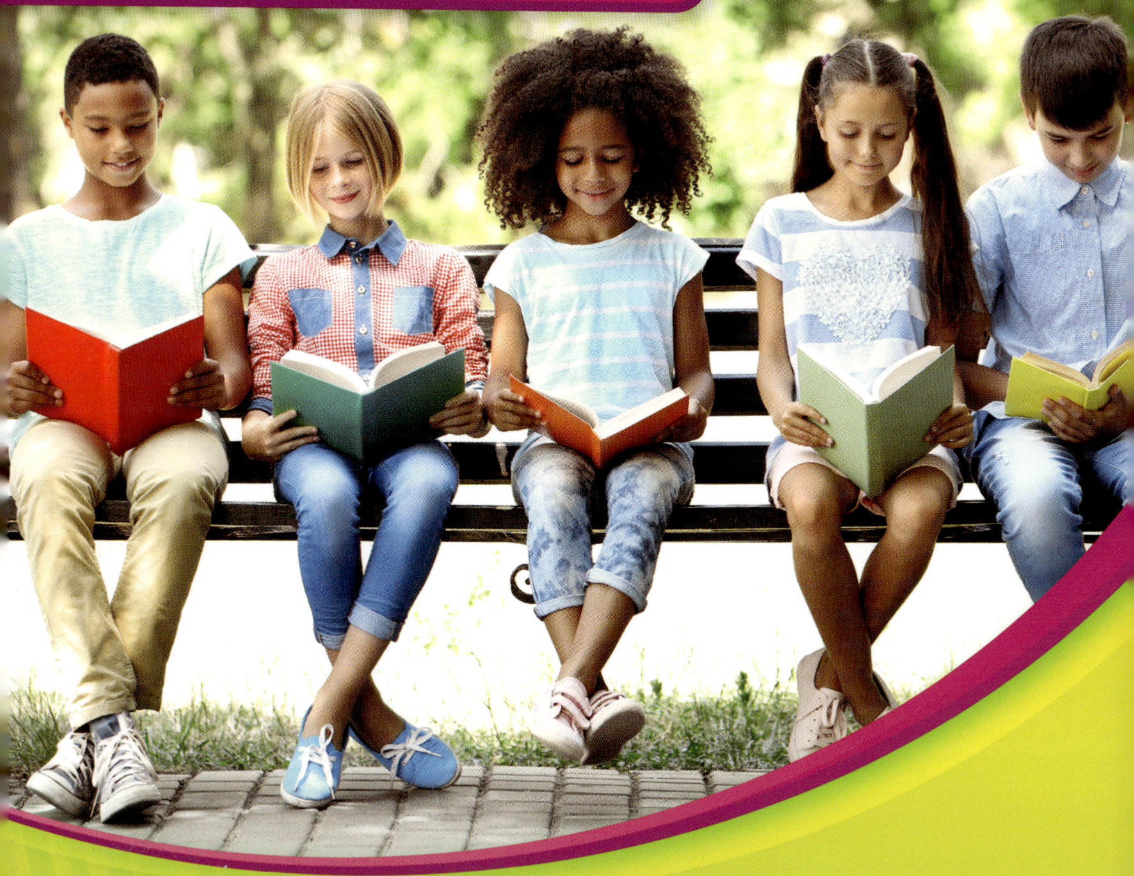

Books are full of fun stories and facts. They help people learn new things.

People of all ages enjoy reading books!

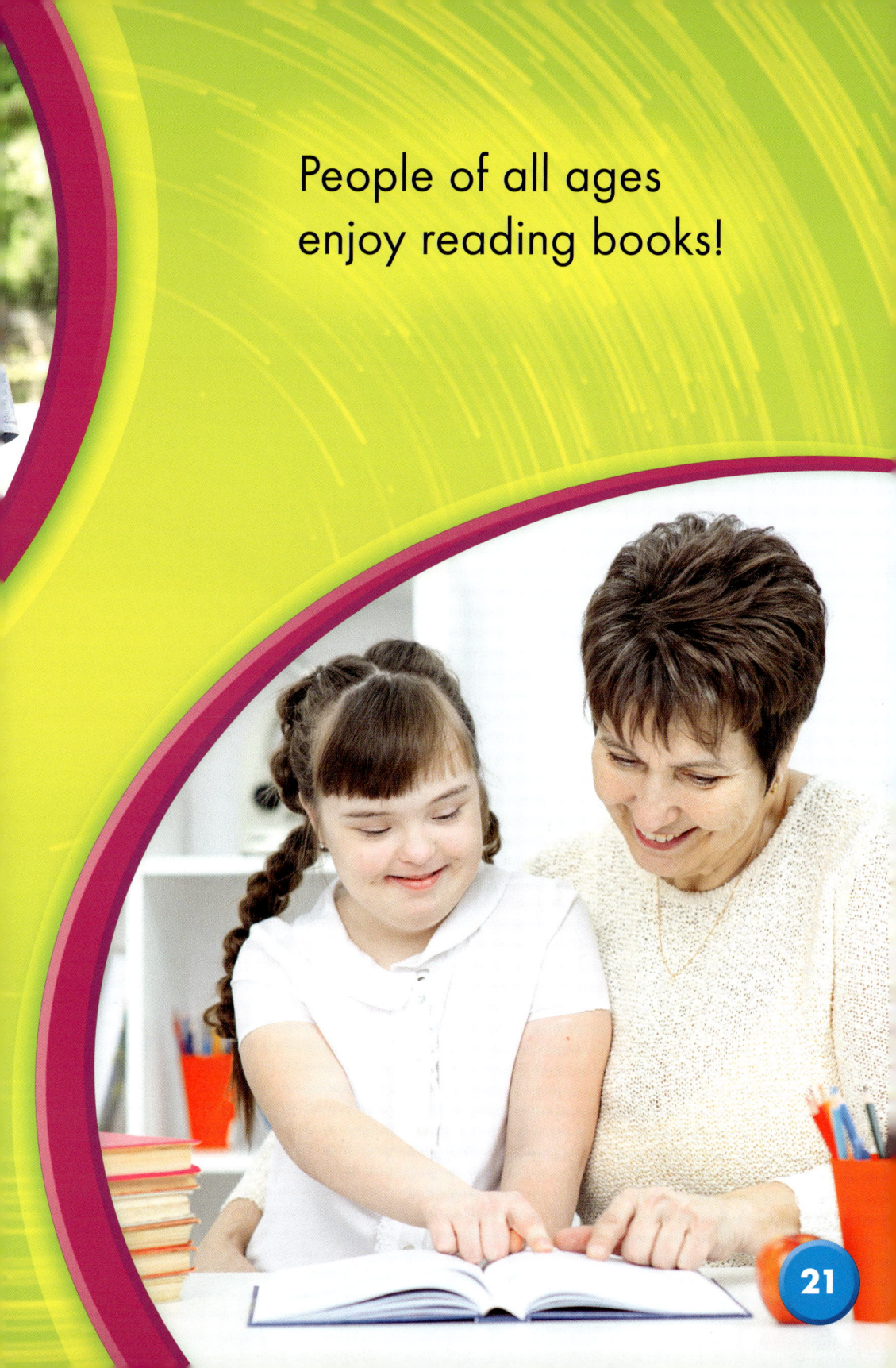

Glossary

bindery—a place where the pages of a book are put together

layout—the order or design of something

printing press—a machine that makes copies of text and images

signatures—units of a book that are folded; signatures include several pages of the book.

trimmer—a machine that cuts the folded edges of signatures

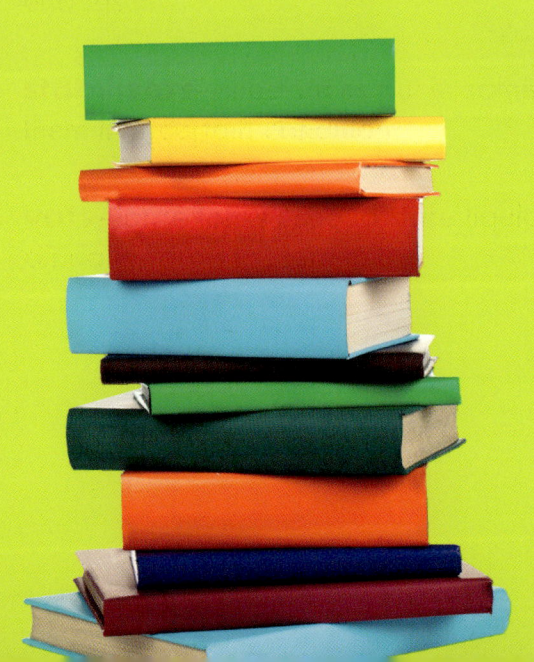

To Learn More

AT THE LIBRARY

Deutsch, Libby. *The Everyday Journeys of Ordinary Things.* Tulsa, Okla.: Kane Miller, 2019.

Grack, Rachel. *Tree to Paper.* Minneapolis, Minn.: Bellwether Media, 2020.

Hansen, Grace. *How Is a Book Made?* Minneapolis, Minn.: Abdo Kids, 2018.

ON THE WEB

FACTSURFER

Factsurfer.com gives you a safe, fun way to find more information.

1. Go to www.factsurfer.com.
2. Enter "paper to book" into the search box and click 🔍.
3. Select your book cover to see a list of related content.

Index

bindery, 12
binding books, 15
binding machine, 12, 13, 14
covers, 18
edge, 14, 17
factories, 5, 6
facts, 20
first book, 5
folding machine, 10
ink, 8
layout, 6
pages, 6, 7, 8, 16, 18
plates, 6, 7, 8
printing press, 8, 9
read, 18, 21

sheets of paper, 5, 8, 10, 11
signatures, 11, 12, 14, 15, 16, 17
steps, 19
stories, 20
tree usage, 9
trimmer, 17

The images in this book are reproduced through the courtesy of: tanuha2001, front cover (book); Senata, front cover (paper); Pisfive, p. 3; wavebreakmedia, pp. 4-5; Moreno Soppelsa, pp. 6-7, 8-9, 19 (steps 1 and 2); PhotoStock-Israel/ Alamy, p. 7; zefart, pp. 8, 12, 18, 19 (step 6); Prill, pp. 10-11; johnnyscriv, p. 11; PapaBear, pp. 12-13, 15 (binding machine); Marijus Auruskevicius, pp. 14-15, 19 (step 4); vvvproduct, p. 15 (staples); Zalepuga, p. 15 (thread); yanami, p. 15 (glue); Hunter Bliss Images, pp. 16, 19 (step 3); Paolo_Toffanin, pp. 16-17, 19 (step 5); Africa Studio, pp. 20-21; Ermolaeva Olga 84, p. 21; Vitalina Rybakova, p. 22.